IDEA WISE Yards & Gardens

Inspiration & Information
for the Do-It-Yourselfer

Nancy Baldrica

Creative Publishing
international

CHANHASSEN, MINNESOTA
www.creativepub.com

Creative Publishing international

Printed in China

10 9 8 7 6 5 4 3 2

President/CEO: Ken Fund
Vice President/Publisher: Linda Ball
Vice President/Retail Sales & Marketing: Kevin Haas

Executive Editor: Bryan Trandem
Creative Director: Tim Himsel
Managing Editor: Michelle Skudlarek
Editorial Director: Jerri Farris

Lead Editor: Nancy Baldrica
Copy Editor: Linnéa Christensen
Art Director: Pamela Griffith
Mac Designer: Jon Simpson
Technical Illustrator: Earl Slack
Project Manager: Tracy Stanley
Photo Researcher: Julie Caruso
Director of Production Services: Kim Gerber
Production Manager: Stasia Dorn

IdeaWise: Yards & Gardens

Library of Congress Cataloging-in-Publication Data

Baldrica, Nancy.
  Yards & gardens : inspiration & information for the do-it-your-selfer / Nancy Baldrica.-- Yards and gardens
    p. cm.
  ISBN 1-58923-159-7 (sc)
  1. Landscape gardening. 2. Garden structures--Design and construction. 3. Garden ornaments and furniture--Design and construction. 4. Do-it-yourself work. I. Title.
  SB473.B34 2004
  712'.6--dc22
                                        2004006029

Table of Contents

Introduction

You can see it now. A fabulously landscaped front yard, complete with perennial gardens and a brick pathway leading to an open-air porch that offers comfortable seating for family and friends. On the side, a pergola-lined walk follows a stream that empties into a pond, dancing with the sound of a waterfall. The backyard has a multilevel deck that looks over the pool and French doors that lead to the family room....

Or maybe you just dream of getting rid of lawn-mowing chores.

No matter how you see your ideal yard, if you're considering a landscaping project, you're not alone. With the resurgence of cocooning, homeowners are putting more time and energy into creating the ultimate destination—home.

Before you can get started, however, you have to decide where to devote your time, energy, and budget. That's where *IdeaWise Yards & Gardens* can help. This book is like a designer's showcase of landscaping ideas, from small projects to large additions. So even if you just want to update your current landscape features, you'll find information on new materials and techniques that can make your job easier.

You'll also find industry terms, tips from professional landscape designers, and easy-to-complete project ideas to help move your project along. When you're ready to get started, you'll also find a handy resource guide for products and services.

Your Landscaping Plan

A yard can be so much more than grass. Well-planned landscaping unites indoor and outdoor spaces, resolves yard and garden problems, and provides creative opportunities for your family to relax and have fun. With that in mind, you'll find that landscaping projects usually are undertaken for one of two reasons: function or beauty.

Functional landscaping creates privacy, screens out noise or unpleasant views, corrects problem areas in the yard, constructs better walkways and driveways, adds living space, or minimizes yard maintenance. Aesthetic landscaping creates pleasant views from inside your home, adds architectural interest outside your home, enhances curb appeal, or indulges a hobby.

An ideal landscape usually includes both functional and aesthetic features, located throughout the yard. *IdeaWise Yards & Gardens* helps you decide what you want where, by examining how various parts of your landscape are used.

Front yards, stoops, porticos, porches, and lawns are used to greet and send off guests. Patios, courtyards, terraces, and decks are used for outdoor dining and entertaining. Pools and sports courts are fun-and-games centers for family and friends. Hot tubs, meditation gardens, intimate gardens, collections, and gazebos are private retreats for rest and relaxation. Sheds and lean-tos are used to store and recycle yard and garden materials. Garden paths and stairways connect outdoor rooms.

You don't have to be a landscape architect or designer to create a beautiful outdoor home. *IdeaWise Yards & Gardens* gives you hundreds of ideas to get started. Each area of the yard is given special attention, with landscaping and decorative details called out, to give you more options.

Planning

Before you begin an outdoor home project, take a look at your particular landscaping needs and desires. Maybe you'd like more privacy on your patio. Perhaps the grass under a big pine tree won't grow. Maybe you'd love a big, beautiful garden.

Do a little research. Take a look at neighboring yards and natural sites. Consider how your project will feel in the area. Your landscape should blend into surrounding areas. It's also important to consider neighborhood covenants and local building codes.

Last, make a site map and bubble plan of your yard and landscaping plans. These sketches will make purchasing materials and working with designers much easier. Color copies of your plans will allow you to try several landscaping plans before deciding on one.

Problem areas can be resolved with creative landscaping solutions. Terra cotta pipe on this hillside provides interesting texture and color and helps prevent soil erosion.

Tame a slope with landscaping. Here, natural stone is used to handle a slope—in a retaining wall and steps.

Mixing materials in unexpected ways livens up your outdoor home, without adding much expense. The mix of brick and colorful tile brings visual interest to this patio.

Budget

Create a realistic budget, and stick to it. It's easy to get mesmerized by the hundreds of options available once you get into a building supply store or yard-and-garden center. Setting an annual budget for landscaping helps you choose materials, plan your design, and stay within your means.

Remember to include plants in your landscaping plans. They'll take a large portion of your budget. If you can't create your ideal yard in one season due to budget constraints, consider dividing the project into several landscaping plans. Or research alternatives that can save you money.

Doing the installation work yourself is one way to save money. However, if a project is outside your expertise, check into local do-it-yourself seminars at building and supply centers to learn the tricks of the trade. Or hire a professional.

Materials

It makes sense to carefully consider the materials, plants, and flowers you'll use in your landscaping project. These elements will be part of your home for years to come. The selections you make and how you use them will impact your project's visual appeal, as well as its cost, installation, and durability. In addition, materials can help you maximize attractive features and minimize less desirable features of your home.

Some projects tend toward certain materials more than others. Decks, for example, are generally constructed of wood, but that doesn't mean there aren't other options.

In general, it's best to choose materials and plants that complement the architecture and construction of your home, and are also consistent with the look of your neighborhood and nearby natural landscapes. Don't be afraid to think outside the box, however. Some beautiful and fascinating designs have been created by mixing materials in unexpected ways.

A yard can be designed to include many elements. This lawn features a private pergola-enclosed patio, cutting gardens, and a small meditation pond, as well as ample grass space for games. If your budget doesn't allow for a complete landscaping project in one season, add to the design over time.

Many landscape designs include a mix of hardscape and softscape features. When combined with intent, the result is a well-developed landscape style. Here timbers, river rock, and stepping stones outline and define pathways and boulders create highlights within meandering planting areas.

Working with a Landscape Professional

You may find there are parts of your project that are beyond the scope of your skills or time available. That's when it's helpful to enlist the services of a landscape architect or landscape designer.

Landscape architects are licensed professionals who integrate the skills of architecture, engineering, and urban planning to design beautiful, functional landscapes.

If you're planning to redesign your property's terrain, change an entryway, or build a driveway, a landscape architect may be your best choice.

If you just need a little help with planning or plant selection, however, a garden designer may be right for the job. Ask to see references, and find out what services your designer can provide. Some specialize in working with landscaping materials, as well as plants.

To find a professional in your area, check local directory listings or contact the American Society of Landscape Architects at www.asla.org/general, or the Association of Professional Landscape Designers at www.apld.com.

Carefully designed landscape features
define spaces and contribute pattern and shape to a yard.

Low-growth shrubs and trees preserve both the Mediterranean style of the home and the open view from the windows.

How to Use This Book

The pages of *IdeaWise Yards & Gardens* are packed with images of interesting, attractive, efficient yards. And although we hope you enjoy looking at them, they're more than pretty pictures: they're inspiration accompanied by descriptions, facts, and details meant to help you plan your landscaping project wisely.

Some of the landscapes you see here will suit your sense of style, while others may not appeal to you at all. If you're serious about renovating or rejuvenating your landscape, read every page—there's as much to learn in what you don't like as in what you do. Look at each photograph carefully and take notes. The details you gather are the seeds from which ideas for your new yard or garden will sprout.

IdeaWise Yards & Gardens contains seven chapters: Greeting and Welcoming, Dining and Entertaining, Recreation Zones, Private Retreats, Storage Sites, Connecting Areas, and Accents. In some chapters, you'll find several features, each of which contains a specific type of wisdom.

DesignWise features hints and tips—insider tricks—from professional landscape designers. Special thanks to Mark Johnson, Niwa Design Studio; Mark Madsen, Bachman's Landscape Service; Kate Ewald, Blue Angel Design; Dann Dickey, Weyerhaeuser's Cedar One; and Peter Lang, Western Red Cedar Lumber Association.

DollarWise describes money-saving ideas that can be adapted to your own plans and circumstances.

IdeaWise illustrates a clever do-it-yourself project for each topic.

Another important feature of *IdeaWise Yards & Gardens* is the Resource Guide on pages 136-139. The Resource Guide contains as much information as possible about the landscapes in this book, including contact information for designers and manufacturers, when available.

DollarWise

Create a one-of-a-kind, low-cost garden shed from salvaged wood and reclaimed windows and architectural millwork.

Search salvage yards, architectural antique stores, and yard sales for unique materials.

Shed plans are widely available in books and on-line.

DesignWise

Mark Madsen
Landscape Designer
Bachman's Landscape Services,
Minneapolis, MN

• Gates and arbors are transitional elements that signal an entry to a new area. A gate offers more security than an arbor, while an arbor suggests a feeling of enclosure because you walk under it, not just through it.

• Pergolas provide a "ceiling" structure for the outdoor living space. They also add a feeling of enclosure. To create a "green ceiling," grow aggressive vines on the structure. Try grapes, wisteria, or Dutchman's Pipe.

• Lighting doesn't just get you from the driveway to the house. It provides a transition in mood between public spaces and private outdoor spaces. Lighting suggests romance, and invites you and your guests to take an evening stroll in the garden.

IdeaWise

Looking for a sport that the young and old in your family can enjoy together? Consider bocce, the European version of lawn bowling. Aside from a set of bocce balls, you only need a simple court to play. Regulation courts are 9' × 13', but home courts can be any size.

Use pressure-treated lumber to create side and back walls for the court. Add packed gravel, outdoor carpeting, sand, or grass for the groundcover. Then add lighting, seating, and accessories to make your court a go-to place in the yard.

CHAPTER 1

Greeting and Welcoming

Your front yard, stoop, portico, or porch should reach out and embrace visitors with welcoming arms. Since the front of your home is the first and last area seen by guests, it's important to create a warm, relaxed atmosphere. Adequate lighting, good footing, beautiful plantings, and comfortable furniture will go a long way toward letting visitors know you're glad they've arrived and you hope they'll stay awhile.

Just as important, however, is creating usable space for your family. The front yard and entrance areas of your home should be places you can enjoy. Landscaping and developing your front yard can create additional living space for relaxing, gardening, playing, and connecting with your neighborhood.

Design your greeting and welcoming area to serve both your family and your guests. A front porch, for example, welcomes friends, but also provides a place to relax with family. A flower garden brightens the neighborhood, but also offers space for hobby gardening.

Think of your outdoor home as a series of rooms, and it will be easy to consider how new floors, walls, ceilings, windows, or plantings could enhance your yard's beauty and function. You'll gain more living space and increase your home's curb appeal and value in the process.

Light up the front entry

with spotlighting and ambient lighting. Well-placed lights at this entryway minimize shadows and maximize safety.

A light situated on the home's façade highlights the texture and design of the brick.

Recessed lighting positioned above the door floods the stoop with light.

Sidelights at the front door create a pleasant glow at night.

Well-placed landscaping can help screen views and noise.
The patio area on the right of this home is screened for privacy by trees, shrubs, and flowers.

Brighten your landscape with lighting

Graduating stairways tame steep slopes. This flagstone stairway provides color, shape, and texture to an otherwise large expanse of grass. In addition, it helps break up the steep slope that leads to the front door. A series of landings provides visitors with a place to rest. They could easily host a bench, small table and chairs, or displays of container plants or yard decorations. Lanterns positioned high on pillars allow light to be distributed in all directions, providing good illumination for the stairs.

Front Yards

Ideally, your front yard should offer a transitional space between the outside world and your home. When visitors enter its perimeters, they should know they've entered a room you carefully designed to welcome them and serve your family.

What does your front yard say about you? Are children welcome to romp on the grass? Do fragrant and beautiful flowers create a welcoming atmosphere that leads visitors to the door? Have you arranged furniture and decorative elements to make a personal statement?

A large garden makes a dramatic statement, but it also requires an investment of time and money. Over time, a garden requires weeding and plant division, but that can be managed. Use mulch around plants to inhibit weed growth, and relocate plant divisions to fill out your garden plot. Choose the proper plants to help keep your garden manageable and healthy. Look for hardy native species. Here, the homeowner combined perennial flowers with rocks, picket fencing, and an arbor to create a cottage garden that blends well with the home's architectural style.

When the front door isn't
visible from the driveway, a
pathway can guide visitors to the door.
A combination of container flowers,
shrubs, and annuals provides interesting
color and texture, plus maximum planting versatility.

*A curved pathway is more in-
teresting than a straight
line. This walkway carves
out two distinct use areas:
the planting bed near the
house and the yard space to
the left of the walk.*

*Setting brick on a diagonal
creates a sense of movement
and helps lead the eye to the
front door and surrounding
landscaping. The brick chosen
for this walkway visually connects with the color of the roof
and the materials of the
house's façade.*

Make a statement

Give a side entrance **prominence** by defining its position with a beautfiul pathway and garden plots.

A dry streambed can double as a walkway. When it's not being used as a pathway, the streambed provides a nice textural and visual element to the landscape.

The cobblestone drive blends with the home's retaining wall, while purple groundcover mirrors the flowers planted on the porch.

Planting flowers at street level extends your yard and ties your property to the neighborhood.

Driveways are often part of a home's greeting and welcoming zones, especially in the suburbs. Make this space more interesting by tying it to the front yard with both color and texture.

Porches

Because they usually have at least one wall, a ceiling, and a floor, porches truly feel like outdoor rooms. Given some attention, these rooms easily transform into additional living spaces for dining, relaxing, and entertaining.

Porches generally stand out due to their prominent position on the house, so help them shine with attractive posts or railings, window boxes, steps, paint, and lighting.

Screen out wind and sound, but not light, with a glass end panel on the porch.

The divided-light panel positioned at one end of this porch mirrors the architectural detail of the home's front windows and door. To screen views, increase privacy, or add beauty, vines or climbing flowers could be trained along the window. A rolldown shade also could be added to provide shade and color.

Color can dress up your front yard quickly. Furniture and accessories are a great way to add a splash of color to your greeting and welcoming areas. Here, lavender tones in the chairs and painted floor complement the yellow siding.

*Design*Wise

Mark Johnson
NIWA Design Studio, Ltd.
Shorewood, MN

Prepare this information before meeting with a designer to discuss your landscaping project.

• Define the project. The better organized you are, the better organized the designer can be. Collect photos from trips, books, and magazines to communicate your inspirations.

• Set a budget. This can be a difficult topic for homeowners. Pick a high and a low number, then settle somewhere in the middle. A local designer will be able to give you a good idea about whether your budget is realistic for your plans.

• Consider value. In general, if you are spending 10-15 percent, relative to your home's

value, you are using safe landscape planning. For homeowners who plan to be in their home less than 3-5 years, it's wise to consult a realtor about the estimated resale value of a planned project. Homeowners who plan to be in their home 10 years or more can afford to spend more on a landscape addition even though it may not pay off in resale later. A swimming pool is a great example.

• Collect any plans you may have of your home and property. Your designer will need a certificate of survey to clearly identify your property's boundaries. He or she will also have to know where gas, water, power, and cable lines are buried in the yard.

• Know your style. Hire a designer who understands your style and with whom you can work comfortably. You want a symbiotic relationship, based on trust and comfort, to make your project fun. There are plenty of good designers out there, select one that matches your style and tastes.

Curved lines embrace visitors and welcome them to your property. The fence, stair rails, and second-story bay window of this home open out toward the walkway, creating a warm, friendly greeting area.

Repetition is a strong design element. This porch features a short railing that spans the width of the home. The fence also features balusters and rails that match the porch. Cutout diamonds in the fence design are suggested in the portico.

Repeat architectural cues from the house

Architectural details can tie design elements together. This home features matching white railings on the rooftop, window, porch, and arbor.

An arbor placed above an open porch provides a sense of enclosure and shade, while allowing cool breezes and fragrant scents to blow across gatherings, through the French doors, and into the house.

Vines trained on the structure provide added shade and privacy.

Porticos

Somewhere between a porch and an awning is the portico. A portico is like an umbrella extended to a friend. It sits over the doorway to shelter visitors from sun, rain, and snow, while they wait at your door.

Traditionally, porticos are doorway arches supported by columns. Today, however, you're likely to find porticos built into the architecture of the front entrance or suggested with other elements, such as arbors or awnings. Either way, the addition of a portico over a front door or stoop adds an architectural element to your home's façade that can help establish the mood of your greeting and welcoming areas.

If your home already has a portico, it doesn't take much to transform the structure into a small porch. Add attractive lighting or a small table to make the space more functional. Expand the stoop and add screening elements to provide room for a small table and a chair.

Interesting posts and balustrades go a long way toward dressing up this home's hidden entryway. Scrolled millwork on the portico calls attention to the door. The white millwork adds architectural detail to the home's façade, while red steps and brickwork add texture and color to the greeting area. Landing areas along the steps provide ideal spots for a small table and chair, decorative arrangements, or container plants, as shown here. Although the posts and railings look complicated, they are made from pre-milled components widely available at home centers.

A portico dresses up a front entryway and draws attention to the door.

Adding millwork to the structure helps tie it to the main body of the house.

Details like a half-round window and lights on either side of the door allow light into the entryway to welcome guests both day and night.

This home's portico and walk-way blend seamlessly into a sitting area in the front yard. The brick archway around the door is replicated in the pathway, which was laid wide enough to accommodate chairs and a small table. Container planters are used along the windows and at the front door to create a garden atmosphere, without the garden maintenance. They also make the flowers visible from inside the house. A mission style light by the door makes the entry and sitting area useable even at night.

*Idea*Wise

A fabric awning can provide a quick and easy portico at the front door to offer visitors shade and protection from rain. In addition, the color or style can be changed over the years to update your home's appearance.

Use sailcloth to fashion your awning, adding trim to complement your home's exterior. Use brackets and hardware to attach the awning, and hang it at a slight downward angle to accommodate runoff.

Good lighting makes
the front entrance
safe and inviting.

Double doors set a
symmetrical design,
which is carried out
in lighting and con-
tainer plantings at
the entryway.

Detailed trimwork
draws the eye upward,
making the entrance
feel grand.

Details take a portico
from drab to dynamic.

236

Stoops

A stoop is a small home entrance, but it doesn't have to lack personality and pizzazz. Transform this simple entryway into a focal point by focusing attention on the smallest details. If you're ready to take on a renovation project, an ordinary stoop can even be transformed into a delightful terrace, creating the perfect spot for relaxing, entertaining, or visiting with neighbors.

A combination of landscape lighting and spotlighting highlight the gravel-lined planting beds along the stairway.

Planters and topiary are used to magnify the symmetrical design of the front entryway.

A simple front stoop can be transformed into a grand entrance with a little planning. This homeowner extended the stoop into a terraced front stairway, complete with landings and landscaping.

Extend a stoop by visually connecting it to a patio. This small stoop features red brick that extends into a lovely front patio. Using brick for both structures blends and expands the spaces. A contrasting gray brick is used to create a round "rug" under the table and chairs.

Add latticed screens to an arbor

to create a cozy porch for your stoop. The panels screen wind and sun, add architectural interest, and allow you to hang baskets for flowers or mail. Latticed screens are available in wood or low-maintenance PVC vinyl.

Inset lighting defines the stairway's borders, while also providing illumination for the pathway.

Details transform a **stoop** into a showstopper. This stoop gets its grandeur from a stately portico topper, complete with columns and millwork trim. A lantern lights the walkway and ties visually to the leaded-glass sidelight at the door.

Even a small stoop can offer detail. This stoop features a small overhang that shields visitors from rain and sun. A planter at the door boasts flowers that match foundation plantings.

Dress up simple stoops with details. The arbor above this doorway features millwork and lattice to accent the structure, which is painted white to match the house. Luxurious plantings and brickwork complete the picture.

CHAPTER 2

Outdoor Dining and *Entertaining*

Patios, courtyards, terraces, and decks invite you to come outdoors and relax. Whether connected to your home or freestanding, the function of these areas is clearly defined—to enjoy your outdoor home. They are the perfect locations for dining, sunbathing, and having fun with family and friends.

Make these areas even more inviting by defining the elements that make them work for you and your guests. Do you host large gatherings? Does your family eat outdoors often? Do you crave a dramatic setting? Do you need more privacy?

It's easy to create the perfect setting for outdoor dining and entertaining. Little things like texture, patterns, and plantings can bring a lot to the table, so to speak. Of course, you may want to add some of the larger elements, such as patios, courtyards, and decks, too.

Design a flexible plan that ensures you get maximum usage from your dining and entertaining areas, both now and in the future. A hot tub might not be in the plan this year, but building a multilevel deck will provide more dining space now—and room for that hot tub later. While you're waiting for those permanent trees or shrubs to mature, add a lattice panel to provide temporary screening. You can even have that rich, lush garden right now. Just grow it in containers.

Relax. Life is hard. Outdoor entertaining is easy.

Attention to detail makes this dining area unique yet simple to create. The patio is carved out of the lawn, with inexpensive gravel flooring.

Candles are hung from the rafters to introduce soft lighting, eliminating the need for electrical wiring.

A weathered wood arbor is dressed up with climbing vines that provide shade and privacy. A decorative metal panel provides late-afternoon shade.

Outdoor furnishings create comfort and style. For long-lasting beauty, look for fabrics that stand up to the elements, such as acrylics that resist rot and mold. Choose patterns and colors that enhance their natural surroundings. Here, muted browns and greens blend beautifully with the trees.

Easy-care, potted plants bring color and movement to the setting. Perennial varieties can be transplanted into the ground in early fall.

A small patio easily becomes an elegant outdoor dining room with a little thoughtful planning. The arbor and limestone floor are the only hardscape elements of this space, so the patio can be designed for a variety of uses. An electric light fixture was wired here, but candles or lanterns also could be used for nighttime lighting. The furnishings and decorative elements can be changed as desired to suit the mood.

Decks

Decks are found on new houses and old, both large and small. They dominate the outdoor dining and entertaining scene—and with good reason. A great deck is more than just a raised platform. It's a whole new level for your home. It just happens to be outside.

Large pillars, with millwork trim, make this deck feel elegant. The steps feature painted risers and natural wood treads, which are echoed in the deck's railing design. The posts and railings—even the posts and beams for the deck above—are white to complement the house trim. These elements, paired with white furnishings and accessories, give the deck a clean, fresh look.

By designing the deck around an established tree, this homeowner took advantage of natural afternoon shade and cool breezes.

This version of a multilevel deck unites two separate decking areas with a stairway. The upper deck provides a secluded spot for sunbathing, while the lower deck offers a space for gathering with friends and family.

Combining a deck with a patio doubles your dining and entertaining possibilities. Brick laid next to a deck invites guests to step down to the patio.

A pergola provides shade for dining, while the open-air deck allows for sunning.

Two sets of French doors make it easy for guests to access the deck and hosts to serve the food and beverages.

New Choices for Decking, Walkways, Boardwalks, and Rails

Beginning in January 2004, the Environmental Protection Agency (EPA) banned traditional CCA-treated lumber, a product that was pressure treated with a solution of copper, chromium, and arsenic to prevent rot and insect damage. Studies revealed that arsenic leaching posed a health hazard. As a result, the wood treatment industry voluntarily moved away from CCA treatment to alternative treatments that use organic, copper-based formulas.

The introduction of new chemicals in treated lumber means you no longer have to worry about the risks of arsenic in treated lumber. But there are also other options available.

One popular new option is engineered wood—a composite of recycled plastic and natural wood fibers, such as oak or cedar.

The benefit of these new products is their outstanding durability and low-maintenance upkeep. Most require no sealing, staining, or painting, which makes them a good choice for decks, walkways, boardwalks, rails, stairs, playground equipment, and outdoor furniture. They can be painted to match your home's exterior, and they are highly durable, withstanding the effects of rain, sand, salt, rot, pests, and heavy foot traffic.

Weyerhaeuser markets a line of engineered wood products under the ChoiceDek® name. ChoiceDek contains natural wood fibers, so it starts out with a warm, rich wood tone that turns driftwood gray over time. Available in two standard sizes, 5/4" × 6" and 2" × 6", and lengths from 8' to 20', the product can be cut, sawed, and hammered like traditional wood.

For those homeowners who desire a traditional wood option, western red cedar provides a combination of aesthetic appeal and strength for outdoor applications. It has a rich color, smooth grain, and natural ability to withstand pests and moisture. Its composition doesn't require chemical preservatives to maintain its attractive properties, which makes it a good choice for decking, siding, paneling, trim, and landscape features, such as fences, gates, arbors, bridges, gazebos, furniture, and playground equipment.

Built-in, raised planters serve double-duty on this deck. They bring color and movement to the dining and entertaining area, and they serve as a backdrop to the built-in benches. Their elevation also helps block wind and noise for guests gathered on the lower level.

A pergola unifies the kitchen and frames the deck.

A corner bench gives cooks a chance to relax and mingle with guests.

An outdoor kitchen transforms a deck into an outdoor living space for easy entertaining. Designing built-in storage and cutting areas in the kitchen allows cooks to prepare and serve food with ease.

Adding a pergola, trellis, or arbor roof transforms a deck

This deck features a full-sized, gazebo-style roof, which is slatted to filter sun and wind. Rather than just roofing one section of the deck, this design creates one large outdoor room that feels more intimate than an open-air deck.

Patios

Create a focal point

by tinting, stamping, painting or inlaying an aggregate concrete floor with a dramatic design. Here, a sunburst design was inlaid into a plain patio floor.

Traditionally, you'd expect to find a patio adjoined to an exterior wall of a house. More and more often, however, you'll find a patio carved out of the lawn as a private spot for enjoying nature and friends. In fact, any place that offers a smooth, level surface for outdoor entertaining is a likely spot for a patio.

Maybe that's because patios are easy to build and maintain, and they're a relatively inexpensive home addition.

No longer second fiddle to decks and porches, patios have been dressed up for outdoor entertaining with built-ins, awnings, arbors, pillars, and posts. Take a second look.

This patio design looks elegant, but it's created from a few simple elements. An overhead pergola helps enclose the space and provides filtered shade. A raised wall provides boundaries for the patio and serves as secondary space for plants, serving dishes, or extra seating, as required.

Create what nature doesn't supply

Supply your own shade with an arbor or pergola over the patio. The slatted roof allows sun and breezes to reach the patio, yet offers the shade that can be sorely missing in new housing developments. Painting the structure to match the house trim establishes it as an architectural element of the home so it will fit in, even after trees mature.

Connect the patio to the yard for more versatility. An arbor can expand your entertaining area to the yard for an evening of dining and games.

Built-in planting areas
soften the hard edges of
the brick flooring.

Separate areas are designated
for grilling and dining, keeping hot, smoky areas away
from guests.

An arbor ties the patio to the
yard, so adults and children
can interact easily.

Courtyards

Courtyards are private, enclosed spaces, nestled within the outside walls of your home. They are enticing rooms, gated from the outside world. Something about them makes you want to peek inside the door to the private sanctuary that lies beyond.

Because they feel elegant, you might assume they're expensive to build. Luckily, you'd be wrong. A courtyard can be built for about the cost of a standard deck.

So go ahead, indulge. When you discover that the hard floor surface of a courtyard virtually eliminates yard maintenance, you'll really feel like you're living the good life.

Look for an outside location that is adjacent to one or more walls of your home. Ideally, the courtyard should also be visible and accessible from inside the house. Enclosed front yards and small backyards are both popular spots for courtyards. In addition, on small city lots where both space and privacy are at a premium, courtyards are ideal yard solutions.

Fountains are often featured in courtyards. Why not create an eye-catching piece of art by going one step further? This fountain was set with decorative ceramic tile that makes a dramatic statement in the flagstone and concrete courtyard. Tile accents are also included on the courtyard wall, at right, which doubles as seating.

*Dollar*Wise

Fool the eye with an inexpensive, painted linoleum or canvas floor rug, rather than a permanently installed mosaic tile or brick-work floor. Use outdoor paint to create a design on canvas or the back of the flooring material, then cover the surface with a polyurethane finish to protect it from wear.

Transform a small, fenced-in backyard into a cozy, private courtyard.

A tile floor lends an old-world feel to a courtyard. Here, border and accent tile add visual interest.

A worn wood-panel fence was adorned with latticed panels painted a cheery green.

A raised garden bed was included as an accent and filled with low-maintenance petunias that help soften the hard edges of the brick.

Create a courtyard by adding walls to a patio. A tiered tile wall encloses this space and makes it feel more intimate than an open-air patio. The flooring tile matches the walls. Accent tiles are added under the dining area for impact.

Terraces

Terraces are simply raised patios. You might find one on a flat rooftop or over a garage. Because of their height, they naturally attract attention, giving you the opportunity to create a dramatic focal point for your home.

Include architecturally interesting details in railings, balustrades, and posts. Consider an arbor or pergola to create a roof. A fabric shade positioned overhead or to one side of the terrace can provide privacy and protection from wind or sun. French doors can connect a terrace to an interior room.

A terrace is also the perfect place for comfortable furniture, planters and flowers, and sculptural details that can be viewed from inside the house. Choose fabrics and colors that complement your home's interior and extend your living space to the terrace outside.

Include sturdy handrails on terraces. Since the rails will be seen as an architectural element of the house, it makes sense to choose posts and rails that complement your home's façade.

This terrace garden
brings a piece of the
country to the city.
Container planters are home
to easy-care perennials and
native grasses.

*Flowering vines trained to
grow up a pergola's posts
help block wind, provide
additional shade, and add
color and movement to the
stark cityscape.*

IdeaWise

When a terrace is located off the kitchen, add
a container garden of fresh herbs and vegetables for cooking. Make your own collection of
mosaic planters with terra cotta pots, broken
ceramic tiles, adhesive, and grout. Position and
adhere tiles below the pot's lip, then fill spaces
with grout. Finish the pot with a sealer. When cooler
temperatures prevail, bring the pretty pots inside for
the winter.

Connect spaces with complementary colors

A terrace wall must provide security, but it doesn't have to block views. This adobe-style wall was designed with block windows that help connect the terrace to the distant surroundings.

DesignWise

Kate Ewald
Blue Angel
Garden Design
New York, NY

Terraces, rooftops, and balconies are often subject to high winds and strong sun. To keep the terrace garden healthy, consider these recommendations:

• The most important consideration in planning a terrace garden is irrigation.

One weekend in a heat wave while you're away from home can kill an entire terrace garden. Install a drip irrigation system that emits drops of water into each planter. Microtubes are attached to an automated self-timer that connects to a faucet.

• Use hardy plants that tolerate full sun. Staple plants include dwarf juniper (*Juniperus*), ornamental grasses, particularly Miscanthus (*sinensis Gracillimus*), and fountain grass (*Pennisetum*). Perennial favorites include coneflower (*Echinacea purpurea*) and black-eyed Susan (*Rudbeckia hirta*).

A balcony comes alive with
container plantings. Many herbs and
vegetables grow well in containers, too. Just
make sure containers receive water daily.

Details create the scene on this lovely patio.
A salvaged wood door is positioned on the patio's right
to screen wind and sound. A solid fence panel blocks
unwanted views on the left. Candles unite the interior
and exterior spaces, and alert guests to the steps.

Combining light and dark
tile on the floor of this terrace defines
the dining area and alerts guests to the
terrace's edge. Raised planter beds provide a nice alternative to railings.

CHAPTER 3

Recreation Zones

Many homeowners consider a long stretch of green grass the ultimate spot for playing football, badminton, or a good game of catch. However, other sports enthusiasts consider a swimming pool, tennis court, or basketball court more their style.

Whatever your recreation needs, a sports court or play area can be created in the most convenient spot in town—your yard. Why pay membership fees, wait in long lines, and try to motivate yourself to go to the gym? Just open your back door to a world of recreation possibilities, from sandboxes to swimming pools.

While considered a luxury home improvement by many, recreation zones are simply areas dedicated to your family's lifestyle. Just as you have separate rooms for watching TV, eating dinner, and sleeping, you can create separate areas for swimming, enjoying lawn games, or playing tennis. The best part of designing recreation zones in your yard is that you can incorporate something for everyone, and you can change the zones with your interests.

Plan for today…and tomorrow

Design with all four seasons in mind. If winter activities are big in your part of the country, leave a large area open for a skating rink or sledding trail.

Today's sandbox is tomorrow's planting bed. When it's no longer needed for digging and building, fill the sandbox with soil to transform it into a flower or vegetable garden. A raised edge gives children a place to sit while they play, and adults a place to rest while they plant and prune.

Swimmers and supervisors alike will appreciate a respite from the sun near the pool. A simple shelter offers a pleasant spot for snacks and time out from the fun. If the pool is used at night, simple lighting makes the space usable.

Provide a perch for pool supervision. Here, a second-story deck extends with a stairway to the pool patio. A large landing offers just enough room for a chair and small table, so adults can supervise the pool action below. The space under the steps could be used to store pool gear.

Pools

There are lots of reasons to love a pool: the dancing water, the sparkling reflections, the cooling sensation. No wonder more and more families are designing their decks, patios, and landscapes with a pool in mind. Wouldn't you love to take a dip after a long day?

Pools come in a wide variety of styles, shapes, and sizes, making it easy to find one that fits into your landscape. Don't forget to plan for a deck and the fence that will be required by local ordinance. After all, you'll want everyone to be safe around the pool.

While you're at it, why not include some additional features that will allow you to enjoy your pool both day and night. Night lighting, for example, can illuminate the water and alert visitors to the pool's boundaries.

Use creative tiling to make your pool unique. This pool features mosaic designs on the pool floor and tile surround, making the pool an artistic, as well as functional, element of the landscape.

Concrete is a popular pool surround because it's low-cost and non-slip. This pool patio was dressed up with tinted concrete and inlaid lighting. Stacked pavers provide a low-walled transition from lawn to pool. The wall spaces and lighting add dimension and texture.

Concrete and brick decking materials are durable flooring for a pool patio. To keep the materials from looking hard or cold, design the patio with curved lines, rather than straight edges. Landscape with flowers and shrubs that spill over the concrete borders to help soften the look of construction materials.

Loosely shaped shrubs and flowers temper hard edges.

This patio features a scalloped concrete edge on the pool, which is mirrored in the materials and design of the privacy fence, pool steps, and planting beds.

A concrete "carpet" is featured under the dining table and around the pool to highlight different use areas.

Cater to both players and spectators

The patio wall is shaped to align with the home's picture window, providing unobstructed views from inside the house.

A rock wall holds planters but could also be used for additional poolside seating, towels, or refreshments.

An open railing allows pool supervisors to see the action, even when seated.

This raised patio allows easy access to the house and provides a good vantage point for the pool. Copying the roofline and wall structure of the home makes the patio feel like an extension of the indoor living space. Steps connect the upper open patio to the pool patio.

Sports Courts

Sports courts can be anything from a stretch of green grass to a fenced-in asphalt basketball court. The most important elements are determining how often your family will use the court, the activity involved, the supervision required, and the position of the sports court in sun or shade.

If your family has small children, for example, a swing set or sandbox should be placed within view of a deck or patio, in a partly shaded area, where children can play comfortably. A tennis court might be located where it will receive morning sun and afternoon shade.

Also consider how a sports court can be used once your family has outgrown it. In neighborhoods with young families, a sports court might offer additional value to potential buyers.

If you'd like to convert a sports court after the children have grown, a tennis court can be resurfaced with brick or decorative stone and turned into a patio. Or turn the open-lawn croquet court into a wooded glade by planting trees.

Yards can be designed with more than one use in mind. Here, an uninterrupted stretch of grass is bordered by a low-maintenance perennial garden. Evergreens are near the back, with hostas in the center, and easy-care annuals near the front. The result is a space that can be enjoyed by both adults and children. Loose-laid limestone is an elegant, easy-to-install edging.

Use structural elements to blend the elements of your landscape. This court features a latticed fence and decorative posts that match the house's gingerbread trim. Shrubs planted along the fence will eventually provide shade.

Plan recreation space for the young and old, as well as the most active members of your family. Stretches of green grass provide room for lawn games that everyone can enjoy.

Enjoy backyard golf for fun or competition. Use poles and flags on regular grass, as shown here, or design a professional-grade putting green or course on specialty turf.

A well-placed hedge can provide privacy and shade, in addition to screening wind, views, and sound from both neighbors and players. This homeowner shaped the hedge to match the fence line.

Make recreation zones do double duty. New flooring options create all-inclusive recreation zones that stand up to basketball, tennis, in-line skating, or biking.

Something for everyone
Design for recreation and sports

Many lawn games can be enjoyed without building a permanent court. Choose a thick, short-blade grass when a lawn is used for play. Balls will roll better, and the grass will hold its shape longer. Plus, it feels good on bare feet.

IdeaWise

Looking for a sport that the young and old in your family can enjoy together? Consider bocce, the European version of lawn bowling. Aside from a set of bocce balls, you only need a simple court to play. Regulation courts are 9' × 13', but home courts can be any size.

Use pressure-treated lumber to create side and back walls for the court. Add packed gravel, outdoor carpeting, sand, or grass for the groundcover. Then add lighting, seating, and accessories to make your court a go-to place in the yard.

CHAPTER 4

Private Retreats

Everyone needs to get away from it all sometimes. Some people prefer to garden, others like to meditate, and some crave a private space to relax and reflect.

Carving out a private retreat is easy. You don't need a large area, just one that's out of the way and away from the hustle and bustle of everyday life. A corner of the deck, a small patio, or a solitary bench can provide solitude for you, your family, and guests. Adding a fountain, pond, or hot tub might be the perfect accent to an existing feature.

If you're creating a new spot for solitude, a gazebo, small garden plot, or meditation garden might be the answer. Creatively displaying art collections, pottery, or antiques also can bring joy to everyone who passes through the garden.

Combine elements, embellish sites, or pare things down to basics. A private retreat should evolve over time—just as you and your family do.

The pergola overhead offers shade and creates a sense of enclosure while adding to the retreat's privacy.

A retaining wall behind the bench adds to the site's peacefulness by blocking noise and wind.

A bench added near a pond and pathway gives gardeners and visitors a place to stop and enjoy the landscape. This retreat is situated down some garden stairs and off the beaten path, which helps create privacy.

Setting the retreat into established trees gives it a feeling of enclosure, while protecting the area from sun and wind.

A latticed screen behind the patio blocks winds and noise and creates privacy.

The raised platform distinguishes the retreat area from the surrounding landscape and provides the opportunity to add a solid floor underfoot.

A private retreat can be one part of another garden area. This bench and pond are nestled below a walkway, above. The pergola frame creates a wall of windows and a doorway to the private spot.

Dress up a section of fence with simple elements to create a cozy private retreat.

Lattice panels, decorative millwork pieces, birdhouses, and a garden gate were attached to a panel fence to create a backdrop for a table setting.

Sunshine lights the top of the fence, so full- to partial-sun plants, such as petunias, are grown there.

Planting boxes were attached to the top of the fence and behind the gate's "window," so vegetation could grow in unexpected places.

The garden's floor is covered in full to partial shade, so hostas are featured.

A private retreat doesn't have to be created for just one person to enjoy. This spot was designed for friends or family to get away for a quiet cup of tea and some intimate conversation.

Collection Displays

A collection is a personal statement of art, whimsy, sentiment, or preference. Designate a portion of your landscape to collectibles, and share your obsession with family and friends.

Intersperse collectibles with flowers or shrubs, or dedicate an entire area of your landscape to your collection. It's even possible to incorporate collectibles into your permanent landscape. Terra cotta urns can be turned into water fountains, and interesting tile can be set into flooring or walls.

Be bold. This is your stuff. Let it define your space.

Simple patio tiles were stacked to give the arrangement height.

Potted plants and a lion's head punctuate the display.

A collection of orbs in varying sizes and groupings makes a unique garden display.

Collections are more interesting when they're displayed in groups. This gardener grouped planters, birdhouses, and watering cans for visual appeal. The arrangement is accented by splashy groups of roses and zinnias. Center stage is a tiered arrangement of mosaic pots.

Create a private art gallery on a small patio.

The large, colorful pieces on this patio are positioned to be visible from inside the house, as well as the garden. Metal art makes a good garden accent, because it can be displayed year round. Even when it becomes weathered, it displays a beautiful patina.

An easel located in the middle of the patio displays a favorite painting, which can be changed or moved indoors during inclement weather.

Small collectibles can be grouped to make a big impact.

These antique children's items were displayed together to create a focal point in the garden. Cut flowers help tie the items to the landscape.

There's no better place to display a collection of watering cans than in the garden. Set amongst the greenery, their color and texture provides nice contrast.

Use whimsy in your displays to delight visitors. These cherubs look like they are thoroughly enjoying themselves in the garden.

*Idea*Wise

Use a collection of old clay pots and saucers to create a unique birdbath for your garden. Drill a hole in the center of a wide terra cotta saucer and two or more terra cotta pots. Secure the saucer on top of the inverted pots with nuts, washers, and a long threaded rod. Seal any gaps between the holes and threaded rod with silicone caulk. Then place the birdbath in your garden. Paint the structure with acrylic paint and glaze, or leave the natural terra cotta finish. Apply a waterproof sealer to protect your new birdbath.

Hot Tubs

A hot tub often hosts a gathering of family and friends, but it also can serve as a private retreat when located away from the house, placed in a gazebo, or framed by outdoor walls and a ceiling.

To create privacy, use trees, shrubs, berms, fences, gazebos, or arbors as wall elements. Your choice of screening material should be dictated by how much privacy you require, and what type of mood you're trying to create.

Lighting also can help set the mood and ensure safety around slippery surfaces. Spotlights, landscape lights, light ropes, or strings of lights hung along fencing or on the gazebo can create a warm, relaxing atmosphere for nighttime getaways.

Don't be afraid to use color in your hot-tub design. This tub features green mosaic tile, which at once stands out and blends into the natural surroundings.

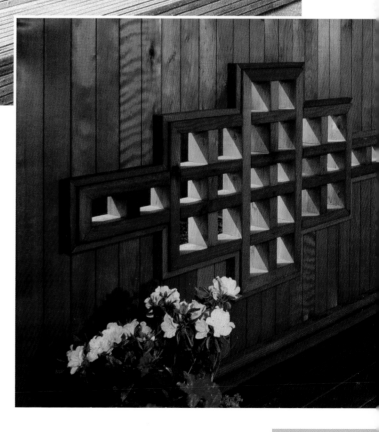

Let the sun shine in. A pyramid-shaped plexiglass roof over this hot tub lets sunshine warm the water, keeps energy costs down, and sets a meditative mood. At night, the clear roof allows unobstructed views of the moon and stars.

Include windows in your hot-tub screening elements to provide visual interest and texture, turning the fence into a decorative element in your design.

*Built-in benches feature lat-
ticework arms that duplicate
the latticework trim on top of
the gazebo.*

There's more than one way to define a space. When a multilevel deck isn't practical, use architectural elements to define a separate use area. This homeowner created a room within a deck by using an arbor and arched wall design. The structure is tied to the deck's railing and completed with built-in benches. Latticed screens help filter sun and wind.

Arches and posts create windows to the deck and landsape.

A concrete patio shaded by mature trees offers a secluded spot for taking in the landscape and sitting by the hot tub.

Hot Tubs

"Be certain to choose a non-slip decking material that can withstand exposure to water. Western red cedar is a common choice."

Peter Lang,
Western Red Cedar
Lumber Association

Consider sun patterns when placing a hot tub.

This private retreat takes advantage of afternoon sun to help warm the water and keep energy costs down.

Meditation & Intimate Gardens

Some homeowners love to garden but find they lack the time necessary to tend a big garden plot. For them, a small, intimate garden provides the beauty and relaxation of gardening, without the big commitment.

Small garden plots can be carved out of the lawn or tucked along a garden pathway. They even can be created in an assortment of containers. Filling the garden with native plants or perennials can further reduce maintenance.

For homeowners who love the quiet peacefulness of a garden, a meditation spot can offer the perfect place for reflection. These gardens are often composed of native grasses, trees, and sculpture. They also may contain a water feature and a comfortable chair or bench. However, it's not uncommon to have a meditation garden surrounded by beautiful, fragrant flowers, too.

Small field rocks outline the site.

Aggregate rock is raked into ripple patterns for textural and visual interest, with larger stones positioned as decorative elements.

A meditation garden can be designed to host guests or invite introspection. This arrangement of elements is meant to be discovered on a walk through the garden. The Asian-inspired decorative pieces and landscaping are minimalistic and natural to enhance the garden's peacefulness. Color is kept simple, with only two colors featured in the landscape, lending a sense of serenity.

*Dollar*Wise

Contact your local horticultural society to discover what plants are native and hardy to your area. Native plants cost less and withstand local climate better than plants that have been shipped from other states.

A beaten path to a private bench is the simplest kind of private retreat. It can be created almost anywhere on your landscape, with little expense.

DesignWise

Mark Johnson
NIWA Design
Studio, Ltd.
Shorewood, MN

• A traditional Zen garden is based on simplicity. Imagination is used to fill in some of the spaces.

• Zen is about experiences, and within meditation gardens we should find expressions of those experiences.

• As opposed to a public Zen or meditation garden, with traditional Asian-inspired ac-cents or themes, a private meditation garden should include elements that speak to you. Look inward and draw from your life's experiences, then reflect them in a literal or abstract manner to create a personal space. For example, if you sat on rocks as a kid, you might find solace in a rock positioned as a seat in your garden.

• A private retreat, or passive area, can often be a small part of a larger garden, a sort of surprise garden. This garden type can be thought of as a pocket garden.

An herb garden is pretty enough to eat. Chives, rosemary, and lavender combine in this garden to become a fragrant—and productive—display. Placing an herb garden close to the kitchen will make it easier to use plants when cooking.

A koi pond provides a quiet spot for meditation in the garden. The Asian-inspired bench matches the color and theme of the meditation garden perfectly and provides an ideal spot to enjoy the scenery.

Gazebos

A gazebo is a unique landscape feature because it's an entire room, complete with floor, walls, ceiling, windows, and doorway. It's almost like a home away from home. Styles range from Victorian to utilitarian.

Gazebos come in open and closed designs that allow you to commune with nature or screen out the elements and insects. Consider your area's climate to determine whether you'd get more use from an open gazebo or one that features screens, doors, or windows. There are even gazebos that feature removable doors or screens.

You'll often find other landscape features combined with a gazebo. Hot tubs, for instance, are often located within gazebos because of the privacy they offer. Outdoor furniture is another popular option, because gazebos provide a secluded, restful spot for relaxing. Some models even feature lighting and heating. With so many options, you're sure to find the right style and design for your landscaping project.

A gazebo situated along a garden path offers a quiet spot to enjoy the scenery.

Incorporate the gazebo into your
deck. This model mirrors the deck and home's
style in railings, posts, and roof. A small bridge
connects the main deck to the gazebo deck.

*Open sides and railings invite visitors to take in
unobstructed views. In wet or cold climates, a
gazebo fitted with windows or latticed screens offers protection from rain and wind.*

*The surrounding garden beds and pathways
are naturalized and low-maintenance.
Perennial shrubs and flowers fill the beds.*

*A simple gravel pathway blends incon-
spicuously into the wooded lot.*

Water Features

There is nothing more relaxing than the gentle dance of waves or the trickle of water from a garden pond, fountain, or stream. Water can cool you down on a hot summer day and calm you down when life gets hectic. In addition, a water feature adds value to your home.

Some homeowners shy away from water features because they think they're too difficult to install, but the truth is that most are very simple, consisting of a pump, liner, and water. Styles range from formal to informal, depending on the materials chosen. Formal designs are usually rectangular or square, surrounded by brick, tile, or flagstone. Informal, authentic woodland designs are often freeform and surrounded by rocks and greenery, such as bog plants.

You can create your own design, or make things easy by purchasing a water-feature kit from a local building or garden supply center. Even a simple water feature becomes stunning by adding landscape lighting, plants, fountains, or sculpture.

Collections of small items get big results when displayed with other garden elements. This fountain pool is bordered with a brick wall accented with a collection of plates and beads.

Almost any sculptural element can be converted into a **fountain** with a little ingenuity. This abstract piece of art was fitted with a pump and placed inside a small pool to create an interesting focal point for the garden.

Even a small water feature can include a waterfall. This homeowner created a stacked shelf from border materials so water can cascade into the pool below. Adding a waterfall to a small pool brings sound and motion to the landscape, which can help block noise from nearby homes or roads. In addition, moving water helps deter insect breeding.

Natural accents arouse the senses. Rock is creatively incorporated into a fountain in this water accent. Polished river rock accents the arrangement and provides a nice textural contrast to the rough-hewn field stones. Brass cranes echo the line of the fountain head and add a sculptural accent to the setting.

Add light to a water feature so it can be enjoyed at night. This small pool is accented with an illuminated water-fall to bring both sound and motion to the landscape.

Waterfalls help block neighborhood or traffic noise. This small fall was built into a hillside. Plant material also helps absorb noise.

Water features can be designed without pumps when you want to avoid electrical wiring. This small pool hosts a water garden, complete with lilies. A pond can be created with a simple rigid plastic liner, surrounded by raised walls of mortared natural stone.

CHAPTER 5

Storage Sites

K eeping a lawn and garden beautiful is messy business. First there's the equipment, then there's the yard refuse. All those rakes, hoes, mowers, wheelbarrows, sprinklers, shovels, seeds, fertilizers, cuttings, clippings, and containers require storage space.

Homeowners often store their yard and garden materials in the garage, but that's not usually the best or most practical place for them. Storing and composting items where they're used makes more sense.

Outdoor storage buildings are the perfect solution, providing both site flexibility and storage options. Fortunately, in addition to the standard metal storage shed, there are many more interesting options. Sheds, lean-tos, and composting sites are now constructed from a variety of materials, in a variety of styles. When you literally think outside the box, it's easy to create a garden storage site that adds architectural interest and functional space to your home's landscape.

Combine your storage building with other elements, such as the fence and pergola, shown here, to integrate it into the landscape. This homeowner even created a small patio space next to the shed.

Provide versatile storage options

A cedar storage chest serves as a storage box and seating element.

A greenhouse is a versatile storage building. In some climates, it allows you to grow fresh produce and flowers all winter, it doubles as a potting shed, and it can be used to store tools and equipment. Building a shed is a surprisingly doable DIY project.

A sidelight near the door lets indirect light into the shed.

Red accent paint on the door and windows makes the greenhouse cheery and bright.

Hinged windows allow gardeners to let off some steam when using the building as a shed.

Board and batten siding is an easy DIY installation.

Sheds

Sheds instantly add function and appeal to your landscape. They free up garage space, store items where they're used, and create an intriguing architectural addition to your home.

Design a shed that complements your garden's theme or your home's architecture. A cottage garden might feature a shed with latticework, salvaged wood, and flower boxes at the window. A traditional home might feature a symmetrical design, with a brick pathway.

This storage building is a nice alternative to a metal outbuilding. It was created from salvaged wood and architectural elements, and blends in nicely with the cottage shrub rose garden.

A small window positioned near the door acts as a sidelight, letting sunlight into the shed.

The door isn't designed to provide security, but it's adequate for securing garden tools and pots.

A light fixture attached to the outer wall allows night access to materials.

*Dollar*Wise

Create a one-of-a-kind, low-cost garden shed from salvaged wood and reclaimed windows and architectural millwork.

Search salvage yards, architectural antique stores, and yard sales for unique materials.

Shed plans are widely available in books and on-line.

A little red shed brightens up the landscape. A flower box adds appeal, as does the window, which also introduces light into the structure. Dual doors are ideal for large equipment, such as a riding lawnmower.

Adding a window box creates a decorative touch on a utilitarian shed.

IdeaWise

Design a foldup table to provide repair space, when needed. Create a box frame with plywood for the table-top and sides, and attach two legs to the front edge with carriage bolts. Secure the folding table to the wall with folding shelf brackets. Use plywood cleats to serve as latches for the tabletop and legs.

A shed can be any size. This looks more like a small home than a potting shed. It features a screened in sitting area, as well as a ramp for garden machinery.

There's no law that says a shed must look utilitarian. This shed features a front porch, starburst overhang, scrollwork, windows, and rails. The structure might serve as a studio or work shed.

A child's playhouse can become a garden shed when its pint-sized "owner" outgrows it. In the meantime, colorful paint makes a beautiful addition to the landscape.

Lean-tos

Because they take advantage of an exterior wall and, sometimes, a patio foundation, lean-tos are simpler, less-expensive alternatives to full sheds. In fact, their compact size makes them the perfect outdoor storage solution for small properties.

A lean-to's size allows you to position it in any number of locations. It can be tucked into a corner or placed along a wall near the garden. Some models are even freestanding, which makes them extremely versatile.

Lean-tos can be used to store seasonal patio furniture, lawn and garden supplies, or grill accessories. A decorative greenhouse lean-to can make a nice architectural addition to your home, and it will provide you with early season blooms or fresh produce.

A lean-to puts lawn games and garden equipment where it's needed. This lean-to makes it easy for children to access lawn games. The convenient yard location also makes quick work of putting equipment away. A cedar shake roof adds a decorative touch.

A place for everything, and everything in its place. A storage shed for wood keeps logs dry and accessible for building fires. This building even features a small area on the right for kindling.

An extended overhang on the side of a shed shelters firewood here, but could function as storage for many other garden-related items.

*Design*Wise

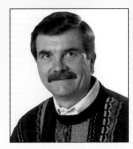

Mark Madsen
Landscape Designer

Bachman's
Landscape Services
Minneapolis, MN

• Place storage structures in the "utility area" of the landscape, not the "private outdoor living space." This could be the space between your yard and your neighbor's property, or an area where utility boxes or air-conditioning units are situated.

• Don't let the storage site become a "throwaway" space in your landscape. Keep storage units well located and well organized, with an emphasis on functionality.

• Group utility items together. A storage site is the perfect location for trash cans, recycling bins, or compost bins.

• Construct storage units to look like other elements on the property. A little beauty, with plantings used for screening or color, helps create a "homey" feel.

Screen views of composting and storage sites

Incorporate storage units into the fence, as shown above, to hide garbage bins and composting sites. A screening fence, right, provides a pretty backdrop.

Simplify. Where space is tight, the back of a fence panel can be fitted with shelving and hooks to hold frequently used items and decorative accents.

Explore fence styles and textures when selecting a screening element. Open-weave fences filter views. Solid weaves block unpleasant views.

Composting Sites

More and more gardeners are realizing the benefits of composting. It eliminates the need to dispose of tremendous amounts of garden debris, and it produces rich mulch in the process. Not everyone wants to watch—or smell—composting in action, however. That's why composting sites are such good ideas.

A composting site doesn't have to be much more than a fenced-off area, but some homeowners prefer to build a small storage shed for the task. Determining how much refuse your yard produces and where you want to locate your composting site will help you choose a design.

Features that make your composting site easy to access when pushing a wheelbarrow or carrying an armful of bags will be appreciated when you're working in the yard. A walk-around, single panel or latch gate are good design choices.

A small composting site can be concealed with a wood box that blends inconspicuously into the patio decor.

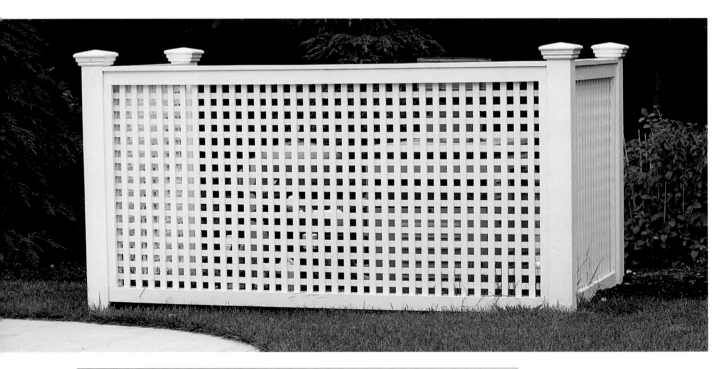

Guests will never suspect that this pretty lattice-and-post structure hides a composting site. The open weave of the screen allows fresh air to circulate around the area.

Composting

Composting is nature's way of recycling organic materials. Items that readily decompose—leaves, grass, and vegetable scraps—are broken down by bacteria and other organisms to provide nutrients and structure to the soil.

Adding compost to the soil enhances its ability to hold nutrients and water, and reduces the need for fertilizers. Compost also makes good mulch for protecting and establishing new plants. As an added benefit, composting eliminates bagging and hauling waste to the garbage or dump.

It's easy to compost at home. Get started with these easy steps.

1. Build or purchase a composting container or structure made from wire, bricks, or wood. The bin should be at least 3' deep and 5' across.

2. Put equal parts of "browns" (carbons) and "greens" (nitrogen-rich) materials into the bin.

Brown materials include leaves, straw, cornstalks, and sawdust. Green materials include grass clippings, fruit and vegetable scraps, and clippings and cuttings from the yard and garden.

Meat, fats, oils, dairy products, and pet feces should never be put into a composting bin. These can result in diseased fertilizer.

3. Turn the compost frequently to speed up decomposition and reduce odor.

4. Water the compost bin's contents to enhance decomposition.

Contact your local county extension office for additional information about starting a compost pile in your garden. You also can access designs and information about keeping pests at bay.

Many municipalities also offer free, or low-cost, compost that is ready to use in the garden.

Compost sites can be as simple or as elaborate as you wish. Here fence panels divide the compost into stages of development. An open site like this is most appropriate in an inconspicuous location.

Camouflage is the name of the game

A boxed-off corner provides the perfect spot for compost or refuse bins. From the front, you'd never know this decorative fence hides garbage bins, but look closer at the extra post, positioned next to the house. The abutment is just the right size for garbage bins, compost bins, or recycling containers. A compost box can be constructed from ordinary fencing panels, available at home centers.

Gates can provide screening, too. This gate features a high, open-weave window, but the solid-door design blocks views beyond—a perfect place to secret a compost site.

Hedges provide natural camouflage for unattractive views, including compost sites.

A low brick wall topped with redwood makes a lovely, low-maintenance fence.

Create an attractive composting site in a corner of the yard. This fence and gate feature solid-wall design, with open-air top, to allow air circulation. A latch handle makes it easy to enter the unit.

CHAPTER 6

Connecting Areas

A yard is a patchwork of gardens and gathering areas until you unite individual spaces with pathways, steps, arbors, archways, and gates to create a flowing outdoor landscape.

Connecting areas are often an afterthought in landscape design, but they should be an integral part of the plans from the start. These are the elements that tie your outdoor home together, distinguish separate use areas, and create a distinct mood for your landscape design.

They also provide concrete value to your landscape and your home. You gain a sturdy walking surface, and you enhance your home's property value.

Any combination of materials can be used to construct pathways and steps for your outdoor home. Be creative. Mix and match elements to enhance your home's design. Provide adequate lighting for safe passage. Lead visitors through your outdoor home with archways, gates, and arbors, and include decorative elements to delight and surprise them along the way.

A combination of brick and concrete was used to create pattern and texture in this small stairway. The brick adds warmth and lends a feeling of formality to the steps and walkway, but the concrete keeps costs down. The straight, square design of the steps and path adds to the garden's formal atmosphere, as do the wrought iron fence and gate.

Viewed from the street, the pergola, which is positioned horizontally, accents the home's façade.

A brick walk inside a planting bed provides access to the plants without stepping through the soil. Red brick blends nicely with the garden's yellow, white, and red flowers. The brick also blends with the home's exterior, making the garden bed feel like a permanent element of the landscape.

Space from the driveway to the doorway is set off with a pergola, and transformed into a grand garden. The scale of this pergola was chosen to serve as a focal point for the home.

The white pergola matches the home's trim, while the plant assortment displays a variety of greens that complement the home's exterior.

Hanging flower baskets add a splash of color.

A dry streambed can double as a walkway when it's time for garden maintenance. The streambed also provides a nice textural and visual element to the landscape.

Fieldstone was arranged in a flowing pattern along this garden's border, laid flat to make it easier to navigate.

Pathways

A meandering pathway lets visitors know they're going somewhere special. It leads visitors to your door, invites them to stroll through the garden, and provides safe passage into your landscape.

Most landscapes have more than one pathway, each with its own function. That function should be reflected in its design.

A front walkway, for example, is generally constructed to last, with high-quality building materials as its components. A pathway that connects garden areas or patio features, however, can be more casual. A gravel or stepping stone path might be adequate there. Consider the mood you're trying to create, as well as the longevity of the connection you're creating.

A boardwalk is a surprising and creative walkway for your landscape.

Planks laid in patterns introduce color and texture, as well as solid footing, for the garden.

The brick walkway and fence wall extend past the enclosed area to invite visitors to explore more of the landscape.

A pathway unites two areas, visually extending both. The pergola and fence create a courtyard atmosphere in a relatively simple design.

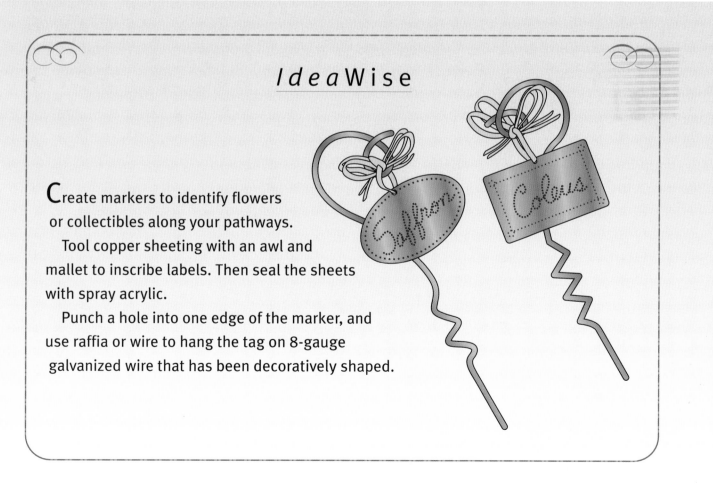

*Idea*Wise

Create markers to identify flowers or collectibles along your pathways.

Tool copper sheeting with an awl and mallet to inscribe labels. Then seal the sheets with spray acrylic.

Punch a hole into one edge of the marker, and use raffia or wire to hang the tag on 8-gauge galvanized wire that has been decoratively shaped.

Use an arbor to signal a transition from one area to another.

Here, a formal garden with rectangular planting beds and brick walkways is connected
to an informal yard and garden area beyond the arbor.

CONNECTING AREAS

Beyond the arbor, loose groupings and tall flowers mix freely, signaling an informal cutting garden.

A picket fence further defines the formal area, as do the neat, grouped flowers and plants.

Stepping stones are an inexpensive alternative for walkways. They create an informal garden atmosphere that recalls childhood adventure.

Nature-inspired stones gracefully blend into gardens. Here, stamps were used to create a leaf motif.

*Dollar*Wise

Create unique stepping stones with quick-setting concrete and a variety of decorative materials. Set the concrete in a mold of your choice, then imprint stamped designs or embed ornaments into the stone before it dries. You can even write names or sayings in the stones. Kids' creations make great gifts.

 *Steps*

A well-designed stairway can make quick work of a steep slope and add a beautiful architectural element to your landscape. Problem areas are instantly sculpted with steps, and humble landscapes are made more gracious with steps that carry you from one level to another.

Steps require two main elements: stability and a nonslip surface. That leaves lots of room for creativity, so don't feel you have to settle for boring steps. Since every landscape and slope is different, your steps can be as individual as you and your garden. Visual interest can be added with tile risers, brick liners, and inset lighting. Textural interest can be created by mixing materials.

Wood deck steps are a nice contrast to the stepping stone landing at the base. The two materials are tied together with color, so that one element blends into the other.

DesignWise

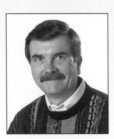

Mark Madsen
Landscape Designer

Bachman's
Landscape Services
Minneapolis, MN

• Natural stone steps are a great way to bring people from one area of the landscape to another. They don't have the "cookie-cutter" look of identical concrete steps, and they cost less than poured-surface items.

• Pavers are wonderful for a "hard-surface" approach. They have a warmer appearance than poured concrete, and they offer a choice of pattern and color.

• Concrete pavers are popular because they can be used to create a quick pathway, and they are easily found.

• Clay brick pavers are favored for their real-brick look.

There's no law that says a bridge must span water. A garden bridge can add dimension to an otherwise flat landscape and tie separate areas together. Used over dry land, a bridge provides a nice vantage point for admiring the surrounding gardens. When placed over a small stream, a bridge offers a place to stop and relax. This bridge was built from wood, which blends seamlessly into the wooded surroundings.

The bridge blends into a naturalized walkway, creating an informal mood. A formal bridge might abut a concrete or gravel path.

A railing is a necessity on a bridge. Because people rest on bridges, look for smooth, sturdy surfaces.

This striking walkway was created by laying dark and light pavers in a diagonal pattern. The concrete steps were tinted to match. The result is reminiscent of a tile floor, but the cost is much less.

Railroad ties and loose gravel steps connect two areas along a slope and eliminate the trampled grass and erosion that usually occur on a hill.

The colors in a connecting
path of loose aggregate
rock call out the colors of
the stairway and wall.

The stairway edges are accented with
potted, shade-loving ferns. However,
on a stairway with more than two
steps, safety concerns dictate that a
railing be included in the design.

The cool flagstone of these steps

is blended with a stacked limestone garden

wall to create an elegant, yet simple, stairway.

CHAPTER 7

Accents

Y ou know how the right throw pillow or picture can make a room? Well, a garden accent can do the same for your landscape.

Great outdoor accents can include anything from furniture to candles. Accents can be placed along a path, on a porch, or in the garden, and many can be swapped with new elements over time, to accommodate your evolving tastes.

Some accents, however, are considered permanent parts of your outdoor home. These include firepits and fireplaces, outdoor kitchens, grills, gazebos, arbors, and water features, such as ponds and fountains. Many of these are built-in elements that require forethought and planning for placement and design.

That doesn't mean you can't add an accent to an existing landscape. New designs are introduced every year, and you'd be surprised how many manufacturers now offer ready-made elements that blend beautifully into any landscape plan.

Glass accents reflect sunshine and add sparkle to the water in this birdbath.

The color of the blue and white mosaic tiles is repeated in the blue flowers planted at the base of this birdbath.

A mosaic-tile birdbath makes a striking accent for the garden, and it beckons birds into your landscape, bringing color, sound, and motion.

Surrounding this small patio pond with irregular rock keeps it relaxed and informal. It also helps the feature stand out from the surrounding patio surface. Tall grasses and water lilies add to the meditative mood.

Surprise your guests with the unexpected placement of accents in your garden.

Hobby pieces and artwork are interesting focal points and conversation pieces for the garden. A bench like this can be made from a cement-board frame, set with broken tile and other mosaic materials in grout.

Firepits/Fireplaces

There's something hypnotic about an open fire. The dancing flames, the changing colors, and the warmth emanating from a firepit or fireplace connect people in a way no other garden accent can. So it's natural that homeowners would incorporate firepits and fireplaces into outdoor gathering places. You'll also find them in private retreats, where people reconnect with nature.

A brick firepit is a nice accent to a wood deck, especially when design and color are thoughtfully chosen, as they are here. The variegated reds in the brick complement the reds in the wood, while the curved design of both the firepit and the bench invite guests to gather near. When a firepit is located on the deck, a thick bed of sand is recommended to prevent heat from scorching the underlying deck.

An outdoor fireplace base doubles as outdoor seating.

The built-in benches on either side of the hearth provide guests with a seat near the fire. Upholstered cushions and pillows soften the edges of the stone.

This raised, flat surround can double as extra seating when the firepit is not in use.

Pillars lend a sense of age and style. Even though this fireplace and patio were recently constructed, the pillars and quarry tile create an old-world ambiance. Architectural antique shops carry a range of salvaged materials for new projects. You can also sometimes find free or low-cost items, such as broken concrete slabs or wood ties, at city park or road maintenance sites.

*Idea*Wise

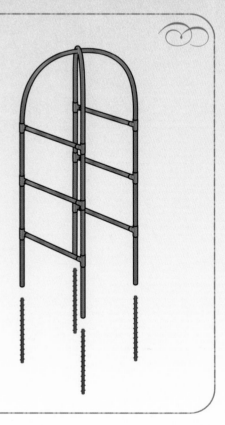

Build an arbor from copper pipe for lasting style and beauty. The metal will weather beautifully to a wonderful green patina and will never require maintenance. Sketch out a design on paper, then purchase ½'' copper pipe, tees, and elbows, as well as flexible copper tubing to create your design. Solder the pipe together, and install the finished arbor by driving a 3' piece of rebar about 18" into the ground, placing arbor legs over the rebar.

A fireplace sets the mood for an outdoor room. A combination of a beautiful tile floor, varied and comfortable furniture, and accents like potted plants, end tables, and mantel displays complete the relaxed outdoor gathering space. The flower-lined pergola above the patio encloses the space and creates intimacy. Varied tile on the fireplace and floor invites texture into the setting.

Mosaic accents in the fireplace surround mirror inserts in the tile floor, tying the elements together.

Arbors & Pergolas

Arbors and pergolas have a lot to offer with their slim frames and slatted roofs. They provide architectural interest, sun and wind screening, and flair to outdoor gathering areas.

While the terms are often used interchangeably, the primary difference between an arbor and a pergola is the size. Arbors tend to be smaller structures, often covered with flowers or vines, that are used as gateways to yards and garden areas. Pergolas are usually larger structures that frame a section of patio or deck.

Adding an arbor or pergola to your landscape immediately signals a separate use area. You might use one to accent a flower garden, meditation area, or dining spot. Choosing posts or roof slats that complement your home's architecture can dress up a simple arbor or pergola and create a special atmosphere for your outdoor home.

This arbor creates a dramatic enclosure for the built-in benches. Redwood construction ensures ease of use, durability, and rot-resistance, for years of beauty.

An arbor/bench combination is even more striking when trained with climbing roses. The bench could double as a private retreat, but the color and latticework of the structure also serve as an accent when situated among the green vines and trees of the garden. A new coat of paint helps this piece easily adapt to changes in plantings or house decor.

Sometimes an arbor is merely framework. This arbor
plays second fiddle to the lush climbing roses that cling to its frame.

A pergola dresses up a simple platform deck, which features two levels and a built-in bench. The pergola gives shape and definition to the structure and filters the sun on a large portion of the deck.

Use an arbor's style to establish the garden's mood. This arbor sets a meditative tone, which is carried out in the Zen-inspired garden. A small amount of lumber and a little imagination combine to create a one-of-a-kind, stylish feature.

Gazebos

A gazebo is a unique outdoor landscape feature because it is a complete room, featuring floor, walls, ceiling, windows, and a doorway. There are many gazebo designs available. Choose a style that complements your home's exterior, especially when the gazebo is close to the house. Also consider your area's climate to determine whether you'd get more use from an open gazebo or one that features screens, doors, or windows. Open gazebos provide a quiet place to relax and commune with nature. Screened or glassed-in gazebos provide a sanctuary from the elements and insects.

Detailed gazebo plans are widely available. Building one requires patience and time, but the skills needed are well within the range of most do-it-yourselfers.

A gazebo set at the edge of the yard serves as a quiet spot for afternoon entertaining. A brick walkway leads guests to the table, letting them know they've entered a special area. The entire structure is surrounded by flower beds, which creates a garden setting in a small space.

Retreat in a public setting. In a backyard that prominently features a pool, a gazebo offers a private spot for reflection. Positioning the building near the pool and woods provides serene views for getting away from it all. It also furnishes a perch for supervising pool fun or hosting a quiet lunch.

Attached to the deck by a staircase, this graceful gazebo provides a shady spot for quiet meals or conversation. The home-owners selected materials and millwork that complement the style of the house and deck. Low-maintenance planting beds surround the structures.

This primitive gazebo was built from rustic wood poles and a wood shingle roof, which blend into the woods nearby. The feeder was designed to mirror the gazebo's style.

*Design*Wise

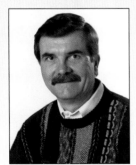

Mark Madsen
Landscape Designer

Bachman's
Landscape Services
Minneapolis, MN

• Gates and arbors are transitional elements that signal an entry to a new area. A gate offers more security than an arbor, while an arbor suggests a feeling of enclosure because you walk under it, not just through it.

• Pergolas provide a "ceiling" structure for the outdoor living space. They also add a feeling of enclosure. To create a "green ceiling," grow aggressive vines on the structure. Try grapes, wisteria, or Dutchman's pipe.

• Lighting doesn't just get you from the driveway to the house. It provides a transition in mood between public spaces and private outdoor spaces. Lighting suggests romance and invites you and your guests to take an evening stroll in the garden.

A screened gazebo is the perfect spot for tea or an intimate lunch. This Victorian-inspired design features a two-tiered roof, scrollwork, and arched window design that bring a touch of romance to the landscape.

"A vital part of pergola construction is ensuring that the posts can handle the weight of the overhead beams. The posts are set in concrete footings you can pour yourself or buy ready-made from your building supply center."

Peter Lang,
Western Red Cedar
Lumber Association

"Introduce a romantic touch by adding a freestanding rose arbor in your garden area. The dimensions of this gateway will be determined by the width of the walkway."

Dann Dickey,
Weyerhaeuser's Cedar One

Outdoor Kitchens & Grills

Wherever there's a gathering, there's food. That's especially true of outdoor dining and entertaining areas. So why not bring the convenience of a built-in kitchen or grill to your deck or patio area?

Outdoor food preparation areas can be as simple as a grill set into a patio wall or as elaborate as a separate cabana with roof, serving bar, running water, and full oven. Large or small, outdoor kitchens and grills add both convenience and relaxation to your dining experience, while bathing your gathering areas in the aromas of an upcoming meal.

If your climate doesn't support an outdoor kitchen, consider a built-in grill to simplify your outdoor cooking. A countertop and storage area located alongside the kitchen or grill can provide easy access to seasonings, plates, utensils, and serving platters, eliminating the mad dash to the house that often takes place as food is about to be served.

Built-in cabinetry hides mechanicals and plumbing. At first glance, you might not realize this beautiful deck addition hosts an outdoor kitchen. The plumbing and gas tank are hidden behind beautiful cabinetry.

The essence of an outdoor kitchen is a built-in grill. This food prep and cooking area takes up a surprisingly small amount of space but functions as an entire kitchen. The grill is large enough to accommodate an entire meal.

A ceramic tile counter and backsplash match the pool deck and add a touch of color to the cooking area.

Storage compartments and pull-out drawers store utensils and plates at the cook site.

A built-in hot plate lets you prepare sauces or side dishes.

Compartmentalize your deck or patio when designing your kitchen. The bold archways in this space accentuate the outdoor dining area while providing a more intimate setting.

Resource Guide

A listing of resources for information, designs, and products found in IdeaWise Yards & Gardens.

Introduction

page 2: shed design by
Walpole Woodworkers, Inc.
767 East St.
Walpole, MA 02081
800-343-6948
www.walpolewoodworkers.com

page 3: cement bench by
Buddy Rhodes Studio, Inc.
2130 Oakdale Ave.
San Francisco, CA 94124
877-706-5303
www.buddyrhodes.com

page 3: concrete patio wall cap by
Buddy Rhodes Studio, Inc.
2130 Oakdale Ave.
San Francisco, CA 94124
877-706-5303
www.buddyrhodes.com

page 11: landscape design by
Niwa Design Studio, Ltd.
6155 Ridge Rd.
Shorewood, MN 55331
952-470-1882
www.niwadesign.com

Greeting & Welcoming

page 18 (above): door by
Simpson Door Co.
400 Simpson Ave.
McCleary, WA 98557
800-952-4057
www.simpsondoor.com

page 19: lighting by
Intermatic Malibu Lighting
Intermatic, Inc., Intermatic Plaza
Spring Grove, IL 60081
www.intermatic.com

page 26 (both): fencing and railings by
Walpole Woodworkers, Inc.
767 East St.
Walpole, MA 02081
800-343-6948
www.walpolewoodworkers.com

page 31: door by
Simpson Door Co.
400 Simpson Ave.
McCleary, WA 98557
800-952-4057
www.simpsondoor.com

page 32(both): lighting by
Kerr Lighting
10 Soper Dr., P.O. Box 446
Smiths Falls, ON
Canada K7A 4S5
800-884-8657/613-283-9571
www.kerrlighting.com

page 33 (both): design by
Walpole Woodworkers, Inc.
767 East St.
Walpole, MA 02081
800-343-6948
www.walpolewoodworkers.com

page 34 (both): lighting by
Walpole Woodworkers, Inc.
767 East St.
Walpole, MA 02081
800-343-6948
www.walpolewoodworkers.com

Dining & Entertaining

Page 40 (above):   redwood deck by
                    California Redwood Association
                    405 Enfrente Dr., Ste. 200
                    Novato, CA 94949
                    888-225-7339/415-382-0662
                    www.calredwood.org

page 41:   deck by
                    Archadeck
                    2112 W. Laburnum Ave., Ste. 100
                    Richmond, VA 23227
                    800-722-4668
                    www.archadeck.com

page 42 (above):   deck by
                    Archadeck
                    2112 W. Laburnum Ave., Ste. 100
                    Richmond, VA 23227
                    800-722-4668
                    www.archadeck.com

page 42 (below):   deck by
                    Western Red Cedar Lumber Assn.
                    1501-700 W. Pender St.
                    Pender Place 1, Business Bldg.
                    Vancouver, B.C.
                    Canada V6C 1G8
                    866-778-9096/604-684-0266
                    www.wrcla.org

page 43:   deck by
                    Cedar One from Weyerhaeuser
                    P.O. Box 9777
                    Federal Way, WA 98063-9777
                    800-525-5440/253-924-2345
                    www.weyerhaeuser.com

page 44:   patio wall design by
                    Buddy Rhodes Studio, Inc.
                    2130 Oakdale Ave.
                    San Francisco, CA 94124
                    877-706-5303
                    www.buddyrhodes.com

page 51 (above):   floor tile by
                    Crossville, Inc.
                    P.O. Box 1168
                    Crossville, TN 38557
                    931-484-2110
                    www.crossvilleceramics.com

page 51 (below):   tile patio by
                    **La Ceramica Nordica
                    Ceramic Tiles of Italy**
                    212-980-1500
                    www.italytile.com
                    www.skipper.it

page 53:   Garden design by
                    Blue Angel Garden Design
                    41 West 16th Street, 5A
                    New York, NY 10011
                    212-727-3725
                    www.blueangeldesign.com

page 55 (above):   Garden design by
                    Blue Angel Garden Design
                    41 West 16th Street, 5A
                    New York, NY 10011
                    212-727-3725
                    www.blueangeldesign.com

Recreation

page 59 (below):   pool revitalization project by
                    Niwa Design Studio, Ltd.
                    6155 Ridge Rd
                    Shorewood, MN 55331
                    952-470-1882
                    www.niwadesign.com

page 59 (below):   water basketball set by
                    Walpole Woodworkers, Inc.
                    767 East St.
                    Walpole, MA 02081
                    800-343-6948
                    www.walpolewoodworkers.com

page 60 (below):   patio lighting by
                    Kerr Lighting
                    10 Soper Dr., P.O. Box 446
                    Smiths Falls, ON
                    Canada K7A 4S5
                    800-884-8657/613-283-9571
                    www.kerrlighting.com

page 65 (above):   fence by
                    Walpole Woodworkers, Inc.
                    767 East St.
                    Walpole, MA 02081
                    800-343-6948
                    www.walpolewoodworkers.com

page 65 (middle & below):
                    Bocce ball set and Backyard golf design by
                    Sporty's
                    Clermont County Airport
                    Batavia, OH 45103
                    800-776-7897
                    www.sportys.com

page 66:   fence by
                    Walpole Woodworkers, Inc.
                    767 East St.
                    Walpole, MA 02081
                    800-343-6948
                    www.walpolewoodworkers.com

page 67:   horseshoes by
                    Walpole Woodworkers, Inc.
                    767 East St.
                    Walpole, MA 02081
                    800-343-6948
                    www.walpolewoodworkers.com

Private Retreats

page 77 (above): hot tub gazebo by
Western Red Cedar Lumber Assn.
1501-700 W. Pender St.
Pender Place 1, Business Bldg.
Vancouver, B.C.
Canada V6C 1G8
866-778-9096/604-684-0266
www.wrcla.org

page 77 (below): redwood fence design by
California Redwood Assn.
405 Enfrente Dr., Ste. 200
Novato, CA 94949
888-225-7339/415-382-0662
www.calredwood.org

page 78: redwood gazebo and deck by
California Redwood Assn.
405 Enfrente Dr., Ste. 200
Novato, CA 94949
888-225-7339/415-382-0662
www.calredwood.org

page 83 (below): bench design by
Buddy Rhodes Studio, Inc.
2130 Oakdale Ave.
San Francisco, CA 94124
877-706-5303
www.buddyrhodes.com

page 85 (above): deck by
Archadeck
2112 W. Laburnum Ave., Ste. 100
Richmond, VA 23227
800-722-4668
www.archadeck.com

page 88 (both): landscape design by
Niwa Design Studio, Ltd.
6155 Ridge Rd
Shorewood, MN 55331
952-470-1882
www.niwadesign.com

Storage Sites

page 92 (both): shed and bench by
Walpole Woodworkers, Inc.
767 East St.
Walpole, MA 02081
800-343-6948
www.walpolewoodworkers.com

page 93: greenhouse by
Jamaica Cottage Shop
132 Vermont Rt. 100 N.
Rawsonville, VT 05155
866-297-3760/802-297-3760
www.jamaicacottageshop.com

page 96: shed by
Jamaica Cottage Shop
132 Vermont Rt. 100 N.
Rawsonville, VT 05155
866-297-3760/802-297-3760
www.jamaicacottageshop.com

page 97 (above): shed by
Walpole Woodworkers, Inc.
767 East St.
Walpole, MA 02081
800-343-6948
www.walpolewoodworkers.com

page 97 (below): playhouse design by
Barbara Butler Artist- Builder, Inc.
325 South Maple St., #37
South San Francisco, CA 94080
415-864-6840
www.barbarabutler.com

page 97 (middle): shed by
Jamaica Cottage Shop
132 Vermont Rt. 100 N.
Rawsonville, VT 05155
866-297-3760/802-297-3760
www.jamaicacottageshop.com

page 98 (below): woodshed by
Jamaica Cottage Shop
132 Vermont Rt. 100 N.
Rawsonville, VT 05155
866-297-3760/802-297-3760
www.jamaicacottageshop.com

page 99 (above): shed with lean-to by
Better Barns
126 Main Street
Bethlehem, CT 06751
www.betterbarns.com

page 100 (above): storage site by
Walpole Woodworkers, Inc.
767 East St.
Walpole, MA 02081
800-343-6948
www.walpolewoodworkers.com

page 100 (below): redwood fence by
California Redwood Assn.
405 Enfrente Dr., Ste. 200
Novato, CA 94949
888-225-7339/415-382-0662
www.calredwood.org

page 101(below): redwood fence by
California Redwood Assn.
405 Enfrente Dr., Ste. 200
Novato, CA 94949
888-225-7339/415-382-0662
www.calredwood.org

page 102 (both photos):
garbage container and fence by
Walpole Woodworkers, Inc.
767 East St.
Walpole, MA 02081
800-343-6948
www.walpolewoodworkers.com

page 104: fence by
Walpole Woodworkers, Inc.
767 East St.
Walpole, MA 02081
800-343-6948
www.walpolewoodworkers.com

page 105 (both): redwood gates by
California Redwood Assn.
405 Enfrente Dr., Ste. 200
Novato, CA 94949
888-225-7339/415-382-0662
www.calredwood.org

Connecting Areas

page 109 (above): pergola by
Western Red Cedar Lumber Assn.
1501-700 W. Pender St.
Pender Place 1, Business Bldg.
Vancouver, B.C.
Canada V6C 1G8
866-778-9096/604-684-0266
www.wrcla.org

page 110: boardwalk by
Walpole Woodworkers, Inc.
767 East St.
Walpole, MA 02081
800-343-6948
www.walpolewoodworkers.com

page 111: pergola by
Archadeck
2112 W. Laburnum Ave., Ste. 100
Richmond, VA 23227
800-722-4668
www.archadeck.com

page 114: deck by
Archadeck
2112 W. Laburnum Ave., Ste. 100
Richmond, VA 23227
800-722-4668
www.archadeck.com

page 116 (above): floor design by
Buddy Rhodes Studio, Inc.
2130 Oakdale Ave.
San Francisco, CA 94124
877-706-5303
www.buddyrhodes.com

Accents

page 122: redwood bench and deck by
California Redwood Assn.
405 Enfrente Dr., Ste. 200
Novato, CA 94949
888-225-7339/415-382-0662
www.calredwood.org

page 129 (below): arbor by
Western Red Cedar Lumber Assn.
1501-700 W. Pender St.
Pender Place 1, Business Bldg.
Vancouver, B.C.
Canada V6C 1G8
866-778-9096/604-684-0266
www.wrcla.org

page 129 (above): redwood deck and pergola by
California Redwood Assn.
405 Enfrente Dr., Ste. 200
Novato, CA 94949
888-225-7339/415-382-0662
www.calredwood.org

page 130: gazebo by
Archadeck
2112 W. Laburnum Ave., Ste. 100
Richmond, VA 23227
800-722-4668
www.archadeck.com

page 131 (above): gazebo by
Walpole Woodworkers, Inc.
767 East St.
Walpole, MA 02081
800-343-6948
www.walpolewoodworkers.com

page 131 (below): gazebo by
Archadeck
2112 W. Laburnum Ave., Ste. 100
Richmond, VA 23227
800-722-4668
www.archadeck.com

page 133: gazebo by
Walpole Woodworkers, Inc.
767 East St., Walpole, MA 02081
800-343-6948
www.walpolewoodworkers.com

page 134: outdoor kitchen design by
California Redwood Association
405 Enfrente Dr., Ste. 200
Novato, CA 94949
888-225-7339/415-382-0662
www.calredwood.org

page 135 (below): appliance by
Wolf Appliance Company, LLC
P.O. Box 44848
Madison, WI 53744
800-332-9513
www.wolfappliance.com

Additional Resources

American Society of Landscape Architects

636 Eye Street, NW
Washington, DC 20001-3736
Telephone: 202-898-2444
Fax: 202-898-1185
www.asla.org

Association of Professional Landscape Designers

1924 North Second Street
Harrisburg, PA 17102
Telephone: 717-238-9780
Fax: 717-238-9985
www.apld.com

Cooperative State Research, Education, and Extension Service
(Sources, Research, Information,
and Local Extension Office Connections)

Office of the Administrator
CSREES, USDA
Jamie L. Whitten Building, Room 305-A
1400 Independence Ave., SW., Stop 2201
Washington, DC, 20250-2201
Telephone: 202-720-7441
Fax: 202-690-2469
www.reeusda.gov/1700/statepartners/usa.htm

National Arboretum - USDA Plant Hardiness Zone Map
http://www.usna.usda.gov/Hardzone/ushzmap.html

Nursery Network
Wholesale Plant Source
114 El Paseo,
Santa Barbara CA 93101
email: customerservice@nurserynetwork.com
website: http://www.nurserynetwork.com

Photo Credits

Front cover: Photo ©Karen Melvin/
Architectural Stock Images, Inc. for
Niwa Design Studios, Minneapolis, MN.

Back cover: (top left) Photo courtesy of
Ceramic Tiles of Italy for La Ceramica
Nordica; (top right) Photo courtesy of Kerr
Lighting; (center) redwood deck photo
courtesy of California Redwood
Association; (bottom) photo ©Brand X
Pictures

Table of contents spread: (top left) Photo
courtesy of Walpole Woodworkers, Inc.;
(bottom left and right) Photos courtesy of
Buddy Rhodes Studio, Inc.

p. 4-5: Photo ©Kathryn Kleinman
Photography.

p. 7: Photo ©Jessie Walker Associates.

p. 8 (both): Photo ©Jerry Pavia/Jerry Pavia
Photography, Inc.

p. 9: Photo ©Charles Mann.

p. 10: Photo ©Derek Fell/Derek Fell's
Horticultural Library.

p. 11: Photo ©Karen Melvin/Architectural
Stock Images, Inc. for Niwa Design Studios,
Minneapolis, MN.

p. 12: Photo ©Saxon Holt/Saxon Holt
Photography.

pp. 13-16: Photos ©Getty Images.

p. 18: (top) Photo courtesy of Simpson
Door Company, (bottom) Photo
©Getty Images.

p. 19: Photo courtesy of Intermatic Malibu
Lighting.

p. 20: Photo ©Karen Melvin/Architectural
Stock Images, Inc.

p. 21: Photo ©Jessie Walker Associates.

pp. 22-23: Photos ©John Gregor/Coldsnap
Photography.

p. 24: Photo courtesy of Walpole
Woodworkers, Inc.

p. 25: Photo ©Getty Images.

p. 26: Photos courtesy of Walpole
Woodworkers, Inc.

p. 27: Photo ©davidduncanlivingston.com.

p. 28: Photo ©Getty Images.

p. 29: Photo ©Jessie Walker Associates.

p. 30: Photo ©Getty Images.

p. 31: Photo courtesy of Simpson Door
Company, Baldwin Hardware Corporation
and Tribuzio Hilliard Studio, Inc.

p. 32: Photo courtesy of Kerr Lighting.

pp. 33-34: Photos courtesy of Walpole
Woodworkers, Inc.

p. 35: Photo ©Jessie Walker Associates.

p. 36: Photo ©Karen Melvin/Architectural Stock Images, Inc.

pp. 38-39: Photos ©davidduncanlivingston.com.

p. 40: (top) Photo of redwood deck courtesy of California Redwood Association; (bottom) Photo ©davidduncanlivingston.com.

p. 41: Photo courtesy of Archadeck.

p. 42: (top) Photo courtesy of Archadeck; (bottom) Photo courtesy of the Western Red Cedar Lumber Association.

p. 43: Photo courtesy of CedarOne for Weyerhaueser.

p. 44: Photo courtesy of Buddy Rhodes Studio, Inc./davidduncanlivingston.com

pp. 45-46: Photos ©davidduncanlivingston.com.

p. 47: Photo ©Jerry Pavia/Jerry Pavia Photography, Inc.

pp. 48-49: Photo ©Tim Street-Porter/Beateworks.com.

p. 50: Photo ©davidduncanlivingston.com.

p. 51: (top) Photo courtesy of Ceramic Tiles of Italy for La Ceramica Nordica; (bottom) Photo courtesy of Crossville, Inc.

p. 52: Photo ©Derek Fell/Derek Fell's Horticultural Library.

p. 53: Photo courtesy of Kate Ewald/Blue Angel Garden Design.

p. 54: Photo ©Getty Images

p. 55: (top) Kate Ewald/Blue Angel Garden Design; (center) Photo ©Kathryn Kleinman Photography; Photo ©Jerry Pavia/Jerry Pavia Photography, Inc.

p. 56: Photo ©R. Todd Davis Photography.

p. 58: (left) Photo courtesy of Julie Caruso; (right) Photo ©Getty Images.

p. 59: (top) Photo courtesy of NIWA Design Studios; (bottom) Photo courtesy of Walpole Woodworkers, Inc.

p. 60: (left) Photo courtesy of Kerr Lighting; (right) Photo ©Tim Street-Porter/Beateworks.com.

p. 61: Photo ©Derek Fell/Derek Fell's Horticultural Library.

pp. 62-63: Photo ©Getty Images.

p. 64: Photo ©Jessie Walker Associates.

p. 65: (top) Photo courtesy of Walpole Woodworkers, Inc. (center and bottom) Photos courtesy of www.sportys.com.

p. 66-67: Photos courtesy of Walpole Woodworkers, Inc.

p. 68: Photo ©davidduncanlivingston.com.

p. 70: Photo ©R. Todd Davis Photography.

p. 71: (top) Photo ©Jessie Walker Associates; (bottom) Photo ©Derek Fell/Derek Fell's Horticultural Library.

p. 72: Photo ©Charles Mann.

p 73: Photo ©Brand X Pictures.

p. 74: (top) Photo ©Charles Mann; (center) Photo ©Brand X Pictures; (bottom) Photo ©Kathryn Kleinman Photography.

p 75: Photo ©Charles Mann.

p. 76: Photo ©Tim Street-Porter/Beateworks.com.

p. 77: (top) Photo courtesy of the Western Red Cedar Lumber Association; (bottom) Photo of redwood fence courtesy of California Redwood Association.

p. 78: Photo of redwood gazebo courtesy of California Redwood Association.

p. 79: Photo ©Tim Street-Porter/Beateworks.com.

pp. 80-81: Photo ©Charles Mann.

p.82: Photo ©R. Todd Davis Photography.

p. 83: (top) Photo ©Kathryn Kleinman Photography; (bottom) Photo courtesy of Buddy Rhodes Studio, Inc.

p. 84: Photo ©R. Todd Davis Photography.

p. 85: Photo courtesy of Archadeck.

p. 86: Photo ©Charles Mann.

p. 87: (top) Photo ©Derek Fell/Derek Fell's Horticultural Library; (bottom) Photo ©Charles Mann.

p. 88: Photos courtesy of Niwa Design Studios.

p. 89: (top) Photo ©Jessie Walker Associates; Photo ©Jerry Pavia/Jerry Pavia Photography, Inc.

p. 90: Photo ©Jerry Pavia/Jerry Pavia Photography, Inc.

p. 92 Photos courtesy of Walpole Woodworkers, Inc.

p. 93: Photo courtesy of Jamaica Cottage Shop.

pp. 94-95: Photo ©Jerry Pavia/Jerry Pavia Photography, Inc.

p. 96: Photo courtesy of Jamaica Cottage Shop.

p. 97 (top) Photo courtesy of Walpole Woodworkers, Inc.; (center) Photo courtesy of Jamaica Cottage Shop.; (bottom) Photo ©Michael Gilimanis for Barbara Butler.

p. 98: (top) Photo courtesy of Walpole Woodworkers, Inc.; (bottom) Photo courtesy of Jamaica Cottage Shop.

p. 99: Photo courtesy of Better Barns.

p. 100: (top) Photo courtesy of Walpole Woodworkers, Inc.; (bottom) Photo of redwood fence courtesy of California Redwood Association.

p. 101: (bottom) Photo of redwood fence courtesy of California Redwood Association.

p. 102: Photos courtesy of Walpole Woodworkers, Inc.

p. 103: Photo ©Derek Fell/Derek Fell's Horticultural Library.

p. 104: Photo courtesy of Walpole Woodworkers, Inc.

p. 105: Photos of redwood fences and gates courtesy of California Redwood Association.

p. 106: Photo ©Kathryn Kleinman Photography.

p. 108 (top) Photo ©John Gregor/Coldsnap Photography; (bottom) Photo ©Karen Melvin/Architectural Stock Images, Inc.

p. 109: (top) Photo courtesy of the Western Red Cedar Lumber Association; (bottom) Photo ©John Gregor/Coldsnap Photography.

p. 110: Photo courtesy of Walpole Woodworkers, Inc.

p. 111: Photo courtesy of Archadeck.

p. 112: Photo ©Jessie Walker Associates.

p. 113: (top) Photo ©R. Todd Davis Photography.

p. 114: Photo courtesy of Archadeck.

p. 115: Photo ©R. Todd Davis Photography.

p. 116: (top) Photo courtesy of Buddy Rhodes Studio, Inc.

p. 117: Photo ©Jerry Pavia/Jerry Pavia Photography, Inc.

p. 118: Photo ©Charles Mann.

p. 120: Photos ©Brand X Pictures.

p. 121: Photos ©Charles Mann.

p. 122: Photo of redwood deck and bench courtesy of California Redwood Association.

p. 123: Photo ©John Estersohn/Beateworks.com.

p. 124: Photo ©Douglas Hill/Beateworks.com.

p. 125: Photo ©Tim Street-Porter/Beateworks.com.

p. 126: Photo ©John Gregor/Coldsnap Photography.

p. 127: Photo ©R. Todd Davis Photography.

p. 128: Photo ©Saxon Holt Photography.

p. 129: (top) Photo of redwood deck and pergola courtesy of California Redwood Association; (bottom) Photo courtesy of the Western Red Cedar Lumber Association.

p. 130: Photo ©davidduncunlivingston.com.

p. 131: (top) Photo courtesy of Archadeck (bottom) Photo of redwood deck and gazebo courtesy of California Redwood Association.

p. 132: Photo ©Charles Mann.

p. 133: Photo courtesy of Walpole Woodworkers, Inc.

p. 134: Photo courtesy of California Redwood Association.

p. 135: (top) ©Karen Melvin/Architectural Stock Images, Inc.; (bottom) Photo courtesy of Wolf Appliances, LLC.

Index

Also from

CREATIVE PUBLISHING INTERNATIONAL

Complete Guide to Finishing Touches

*D*iscover ingenious ideas and helpful how-to tips for transforming your yard into functional and beautiful outdoor living spaces.

ISBN 1-58923-144-9

Complete Guide to Creative Landscapes

*T*ransform your yard into a series of beautiful, functional rooms—real living space, complete with furnishings and accessories. *The Complete Guide to Creative Landscapes* provides information, advice, and step-by-step instructions for over 60 projects that will help you turn an ordinary landscape into an outdoor home the entire family can use and enjoy.

ISBN 0-86573-579-4

CREATIVE PUBLISHING INTERNATIONAL

18705 LAKE DRIVE EAST
CHANHASSEN, MN 55317

WWW.CREATIVEPUB.COM